P9-DEW-356

Tualatin Public Library
18878 SW Martinazzi Avenue
Tualatin, OR 97062-7092
Member of Washington County Cooperative Library Services

GHOSTLY EVIDENCE

EVIDENCE

EXPLORING THE PARANORMAL

KELLY MILNER HALLS

M MILLBROOK PRESS • MINNEAPOLIS

To my kids, Kerry and Vanessa, who make my life
worth living. And to my mom, Georgia, who will
make my passing a reunion —KMH

Text copyright © 2014 by Kelly Milner Halls

All rights reserved. International copyright secured. No part of this book may be reproduced,
stored in a retrieval system, or transmitted in any form or by any means—electronic,
mechanical, photocopying, recording, or otherwise—without the prior permission of Lerner
Publishing Group, Inc., except for the inclusion of brief quotations in an acknowledged review.

Millbrook Press
A division of Lerner Publishing Group, Inc.
241 First Avenue North
Minneapolis, MN 55401 USA

For reading levels and more information, look up this title at www.lernerbooks.com.

Main body text set in Felbridge Std 10/16.
Typeface provided by Monotype Typography.

Library of Congress Cataloging-in-Publication Data

Halls, Kelly Milner, 1957–
      Ghostly evidence : exploring the paranormal / by Kelly Milner Halls.
         pages cm
      Includes bibliographical references and index.
      ISBN 978–1–4677–0593–6 (lib. bdg. : alk. paper)
      ISBN 978–1–4677–4763–9 (eBook)
      1. Ghosts—Research. I. Title.
   BF1471.H35 2014
   133.1—dc23   2013042294

Manufactured in the United States of America
1 – BP – 7/15/14

CONTENTS

INTRODUCTION

For centuries, we've feared them. Ghosts. Spirits. Entities able to travel between the worlds of the living and the dead. They've captured our imaginations and haunted our books, our television shows, and our movies. In those places, we delight in our fear of ghosts. Objects leap off shelves, and sounds that seem to come from nowhere make our skin crawl. But why do we care if ghosts really exist? And what evidence, if any, suggests they *could* be real?

Why we care is easy. Some of us are comforted by the thought that some part of the people and animals we love exist in some form after they die. We want to survive the death of our human bodies too. The thought that a loved one's ghost is nearby may be reassuring during difficult times. But the possibility of an unfamiliar presence can be creepy and scary.

Identifying spiritual entities drives the quest for proof of the paranormal (something that science cannot explain). So far, proof—real facts and not just theories—has eluded us. But evidence that shows something is *possible* is another story.

Most so-called ghost sightings can be explained away upon close examination. The strange light in your hallway that looked like a woman floating was really the headlight of a car driving by your house. Other incidents are not so easy to dismiss.

So, what is the truth about the existence of ghosts? You'll have to decide that for yourself. Read these pages with a questioning but open mind. Amazement may replace some of your fear—and the frauds will be easier to recognize.

Let's look at the most haunting ghostly evidence I could unearth.

CHAPTER ONE

WHAT IS A GHOST?

People who believe in ghosts think of them as spirit forms of those who have died. They think ghosts may try to communicate with the living from beyond the grave. Of course, not everyone believes in ghosts. A February 2013 *Huffington Post* poll of one thousand people found that 32 percent did not believe in ghosts and 25 percent weren't sure. But almost half—43 percent—believed ghosts were real.

New York psychotherapist Jonathan Alpert explains why some people believe in ghosts. "It provides comfort," he says. "If we're afraid of death or what happens after we die, we might create these stories or ideas about an afterlife, or ghosts. I think it helps calm people's fear and anxieties."

Paranormal investigators say spirits can take on a variety of forms.

APPARITIONS

In 1872 John and Mary Slattery had a mansion built in New Orleans, Louisiana. The couple lived in it with their six children and two family friends. P. J. McMahon and Sons Undertaking Company purchased the Victorian property in 1923 and converted it into a full-service mortuary (funeral home). The company escorted the lifeless bodies of more than twenty thousand people to their final resting places. In 1996 the building was sold again, but it fell into disrepair.

With the mansion's history in mind, audio-video expert Jeff Borne purchased the building in 2007 to create a tourist attraction: the Mortuary Haunted House. He uses state-of-the-art special effects to simulate ghostly horrors for adventurous visitors.

Manager Lance Hock leads hundreds of visitors through the haunted house every year. It's creepy that so many dead bodies were drained of their blood and prepared for burial under this roof, but Borne is an expert in special effects, so the thrills are more fun than scary. Even so, Hock and others take pictures of every nook and cranny, just for fun—and just in case.

In September 2007, Hock was reviewing his latest ghost tour photos, and he made a startling discovery. One of his pictures of the mortuary staircase looked absolutely normal, but the second left him speechless. It showed the image of a transparent little girl, shyly peeking around the staircase corner.

Allison DuBois: Medium and Profiler

In the past, mediums were often professional hoaxers, theatrical frauds who used props and special effects to fool the public into thinking they could connect with the dead. Unlike them, Allison DuBois tries to make the world a better place. Known for her work with Arizona law enforcement as a psychic profiler of criminals, DuBois's gifts were so impressive that NBC based its television crime drama *Medium* on her life and family.

Like the character in the television program, DuBois talks to dead people. Her window to the afterlife allegedly opened when she was six years old. After attending her great-grandfather's funeral, young Allison saw his apparition standing at the foot of her bed. When he talked, she listened.

"Tell your mom I'm still with her," he said, "and that I'm not in pain anymore."

This was the first of thousands of messages dead people supposedly have sent through DuBois. She considers this gift a blessing. "I talk to dead people," she says, "and they always have a lot to say. Movies portray it as being dark and macabre, but it's not. It's very gratifying. They look beautiful and flawless—the best they were in life, amplified."

Angry ghosts sometimes express themselves inappropriately, according to DuBois. While staying in a haunted hotel, she awoke to a stabbing sensation in her back. She sat up and saw a man dressed in cowboy attire standing in the corner. He had died one hundred years earlier. DuBois was annoyed, but she felt he didn't mean to frighten her.

"Energies that are darker are just trying to get your attention," she says. "They don't mean you any physical harm. But because they didn't live right in life, it's the only way they know to communicate in death." DuBois believes the living might be able to help these troubled energies fix the things they left unresolved so they can move on.

Did Hock capture proof of ghostly apparitions? Was one of the children embalmed at the New Orleans landmark still haunting it? Or did a living child sneak into the shot? It's hard to say for sure. But if it is an authentic ghost picture, Hock's photograph looks like what most people imagine when they hear the word *ghost*.

Apparitions are common in fiction, but not in real life. Mediums (people who claim to see or hear from ghosts) say that they have contact with them regularly. Ghost hunters, however, rarely get photos or other evidence of them. If you witness an apparition, you're one of very few people who can make that claim.

SHADOW FIGURES AND DARK MASSES

This 1937 photo shows the entrance of the Burlington County Prison.

Built in 1811 and closed in 1965, Burlington County Prison in Mount Holly, New Jersey, has been long abandoned. Electricity is a distant memory within most of its stone walls. Imagine wandering through the prison late at night, one of several people taking part in a Halloween ghost hunt. Rusty prison doors screech when opened. The narrow beam of a flashlight guides you.

Men suffered here. They lived out their sentences for violent crimes. Some were hanged from the prison gallows. More than a century of sorrow, despair, and regret seems to surround you in the dark. There's no sign of the living, but as your eyes search the walkway, you see a shadowy figure that fades almost as quickly as it appears. The group moves on, but you hesitate. *How can there be a shadow if nobody is there to cast it?* you wonder.

You've just witnessed what experts call "shadow figures." According to many paranormal investigators, shadow figures are darker and angrier than apparitions. People who died riddled with guilt might haunt this world as shadow figures. Author and Presbyterian minister Mark Hunnemann says they're evil. "When I saw my first shadow figure twelve years ago, I knew instinctively what it was—a demon," Hunnemann explains. "From head to toe, there is no light emanating—just walking darkness; walking evil."

Jason Hawes stars in the SyFy's *Ghost Hunters*. He cautions that many shadow figures are simply a case of mistaken identity. They are sometimes shadows people cast without realizing they are the source. But he admits that some shadow figures are not so easily debunked.

SPIRIT ORBS

The *Star of India,* a working tall ship built more than 150 years ago, is docked in a harbor in San Diego, California. The ship is known for its history as a trading vessel—and for its ghostly energy. Thousands of tourists visit the ship every day, but in the evenings, paranormal investigators sometimes board.

Fifteen-year-old John Campbell reportedly fell to his death from a mast on the *Star of India.*

Danielle Young has joined a paranormal team to practice taking pictures at night. Several other people hope to hear from ghosts, including the ghost of fifteen-year-old orphan John Campbell. John was a stowaway on the ship when it sailed the Pacific Ocean until a careless moment sent him crashing 127 feet (39 meters) from the tallest mast to the deck below. For three days, the boy suffered. He died on June 26, 1884. With no loved ones back home to mourn him, the crew of the *Star of India* buried him at sea. But his spirit may have lingered on the ship.

"Talk to him," the paranormal experts tell Danielle. "But don't ask about his death. Ghosts don't like to talk about that. Start by telling him your name."

She says hello, whispers her name, and explains she's a fifteen-year-old photographer. Tiny digital recorders are on, waiting to capture any electronic voice responses from John, but none seems to have been uttered. Danielle assumes nothing is going to happen, so she resumes taking pictures.

Before leaving the ship, she and the experts review her images. "What is that green circle of light on so many of my pictures?" she asks the others. The ghost hunters smile.

"It's John," they explain. "Ghosts sometimes communicate as orbs of light in pictures."

Some orbs may indicate spiritual activity. But most can be explained more easily. "Orbs most often appear on camera when a piece of airborne dust, an insect, or a water droplet is close to the camera, outside of the lens's depth of field, and the flash source is no more than a few degrees away from the axis of the camera lens," according to Skeptoid.com writer Brian Dunning. "This causes the object to be brightly lit but way out of focus, resulting in a semi-transparent whitish circle."

GHOSTLY MISTS

St. Francisville, Louisiana, is home to Myrtles Plantation. Some people claim it's one of the most haunted places in the world.

David Bradford completed the plantation in 1797. It was a hiding place as much as it was a home. Bradford made President George Washington angry when he led the Whiskey Rebellion in Pennsylvania to protest a tax on whiskey in 1794. Washington sent thirteen thousand troops to put down the uprising, so Bradford ran to Louisiana until things cooled down. When he received his presidential pardon, Bradford sold the homestead and returned to Pennsylvania.

Ruffin Gray Stirling and Mary Catherine Cobb Stirling lived at Myrtles Plantation with their nine children, but five did not survive to adulthood. Countless slaves also died on the plantation's grounds. Restless souls are not hard to imagine there.

WGNO-ABC reporter Vanessa Bolano hoped to capture something ghostly when she brought a film crew to Myrtles Plantation in December 2012. What she got was an odd mist, even though the region's only major waterway, the Mississippi River, is more than 2 miles (3 kilometers) away and not a trace of fog was in the air.

"We wanted to highlight the history of the plantation, when this thing flew through quickly," Bolano says in the *New York Daily News*. "In one frame, it looks like the profile of a woman's face."

Bolano may have captured photographic proof of a ghostly mist, but experts at PSICAN (Paranormal Studies and Investigations Canada) say it's unlikely. They insist most ghostly mists can be traced to natural origins—pockets of smoke or fog. They encourage the skeptical investigation of all mists, so the few that cannot be explained will offer credible evidence.

RESIDUAL IMAGES

Residual images are not ghosts. They are more like movies of past events playing in an endless loop, starring people who have long since passed away. According to paranormal investigators, some events in life are so powerful that they imprint themselves in the place where they happened. People living today see those residual images—like movies before their eyes—years, decades, even centuries later.

The photo taken by an amateur ghost hunter shows the residual image of what could be a Civil War–era ghost. The arrow points to a figure shown more clearly in the inset photo.

The Battle of Gettysburg was the bloodiest battle of the American Civil War (1861–1865). Fighting lasted three days and claimed nearly eight thousand Union and Confederate lives. The devastation left its mark on the Pennsylvania countryside. Some say residual images of the battle replay the tragic confrontation over and over again. Investigators from *Ghost Hunters* captured what they think could be residual images. They visited the historic battlefield in an episode that aired in January 2014. They recorded heat-sensitive videos showing what might be Civil War soldiers running into the bushes.

"In a residual haunting," says paranormal investigator Dave Juliano, "there is no spirit involved. This type of event is not dangerous at all so if you ever have the chance to witness one, do so without fear."

Skeptics believe residual hauntings are nothing more than strong emotions mixed with vivid imaginations. But how would that explain residual photo-video evidence?

SCENTS

Did your great-grandfather smoke a pipe? Did your grandmother wear perfume that smelled like roses? If any of your dearly departed family members or friends had a strong connection to a specific scent, they might reach out by emitting that aroma. When my mother passed away, I believe a special message using scent happened to me.

My mother loved gingerbread more than any other dessert. When she passed away in 2000, I locked up my house in Spokane, Washington, and flew to her funeral in St. George, Texas, with my two daughters. When we returned home and opened the front door, the scent of gingerbread welcomed us. I've never baked gingerbread, but every room smelled like the sweet, spicy cake. Paranormal experts might say my mom was saying good-bye.

Florida's St. Augustine Lighthouse, built in 1874 and once featured on SyFy's *Ghost Hunters* television series, is known for paranormal activity, including an apparition in the basement, voices in the swirling staircase, and the unexplained occasional scent of cigar smoke. One of its departed caretakers from long ago always smoked a cigar.

Scent can be a tricky element, though. Skeptics say these scents can be explained. What seems to be a smell from the afterlife could be drifting from your neighbor's place. However, it's difficult to explain away the scent of gardenias in the middle of winter or the spicy fragrance of gingerbread when no one is baking.

Animal Ghosts

Can animals be ghosts? According to paranormal investigator and author Richard Senate, the spirits of dogs and cats stay close by for several days before moving on. "Animal hauntings are very common," he says. "It's a pet's way of saying good-bye." Senate believes the strength of an animal's connection to human beings in life determines its likelihood to haunt after death.

British wing commander Guy Gibson was a hero during World War II (1939–1945). His main connection on land was with his dog, a chocolate Labrador retriever. Gibson left the dog only when flying missions against the Nazi enemy—and the dog only left his master to dig holes outside the living quarters. When the dog died in May 1944, Gibson and his men laid him to rest just a few feet from where he'd lived with Gibson.

When Gibson passed away in September 1944, a memorial service took place not far from where his beloved pet was buried. Photographers took dozens of photos to mark the somber occasion. When they developed the film, something unexpected appeared. Sitting between two sections of the choir was the ghostly apparition of Gibson's dark-colored dog. No one had seen him when the service was taking place.

In 2011 paranormal investigator Paul Drake searched for the dog's ghost at the military base, and he said his team made contact. "One of our investigators felt a cold spot, and when we measured it, it was eighteen inches [46 centimeters] tall, which was about the height of the dog," he says.

"I heard the growl of a dog," said investigator Michelle Clements, who was part of Drake's team. "Three of us heard it, and we all agreed it was a dog."

Commander Gibson's dog was popular with many members of the Royal Air Force, a branch of the British Armed Forces. After the dog died, some say his ghost remained behind.

Skeptic and journalist Joe Nickell has spent his life debunking paranormal mysteries. He believes most pet hauntings can be traced to waking dreams or a person's reluctance to admit his or her pet is no longer alive. But Senate stands firm. He insists if ghostly humans linger on Earth, their pets could also be nearby.

TRINKETS AND DREAMS

Have you ever found a small item in the wrong place? Your favorite hair clip or the ring your grandmother gave you? What about a penny or a dime? According to paranormal investigators, finding such trinkets out of place might not be coincidental. They might be a message from the dead.

When Jamie Jackson, director of Gettysburg Ghosts, in Pennsylvania, lost her grandmother, she was devastated. Her best friend was gone. Almost nothing made her feel better—until she received what she called "pennies from heaven."

"I unlocked my office door, turned on the lights, and went over to my desk. There I found three pennies sitting in front of my keyboard, face up and all in a row," she says. She kept the pennies but didn't register how odd it was until the same thing happened a few days later.

"I finished loading the dishwasher and rinsed out the sink," Jackson adds. "As I placed the dishcloth on the faucet, I noticed three pennies lined up on the sink. This caught my attention, because just moments before, there were no pennies."

A week later, Jackson was at a plant nursery admiring the African violets, when she saw it again—three pennies, faceup, in a perfect line. But Jackson was never afraid. "It was as if she just wanted to let me know that she was there in spirit," she says.

Loved ones may also reach out to us when we're not even awake. According to some paranormal experts, sometimes when a loved one who has died appears to us in a dream, it's not really a dream. It's a visit—his or her spirit connecting with our unconscious mind.

I have vivid dreams of my mother about twice a year. She appears as I remember her when I was a child: young and happy. Every time in these dreams, I ask her if she's back or if she's still dead. She smiles and says she's not back. Then she gives me a big hug and reminds me she's never far away. Skeptics say dreams like mine are only dreams—vivid reminders of the mother who loved and raised me. They may be right, but seeing her feels awfully real.

CHAPTER TWO

HAUNTED PLACES

Where are ghosts most likely to be encountered? Strong emotional experiences increase the odds of a place having paranormal activity. If you meet a nice clerk at the department store, it's a pleasant experience, but it doesn't create a strong emotional connection. If you live with your grandmother for a summer, the emotions you share will be far more powerful than that moment with the clerk. One of the strongest connections between the here and now and the hereafter is love.

Anger and confusion are the next most likely emotions connected to ghostly activity. If the cause of a person's death is unresolved or if there were important words left unspoken, a haunting may be more probable.

With these things in mind, consider what places might be paranormal hot spots.

OLD FAMILY HOMES

Some houses have seen decades of history. With the passing of time, ghostly energy seems more likely to collect and linger. The William Heath Davis House in San Diego, California, is one of those residences.

Built in 1850 by wealthy shipping magnate William Heath Davis, the house was one of nine houses scattered throughout New Town, a rowdy area of San Diego. Today, it stands as a museum to celebrate the city's history. The Davis House has served multiple roles, including as a hospital (where many people died) and as a hiding place of a World War I (1914–1918) spy. The house has long been popular with paranormal investigators. Some have recorded the meows of an unseen cat and the voices of ghosts, while others have photographed images of apparitions, orbs, and shadows.

MORE EVIDENCE: THE WHALEY HOUSE

Not all old houses are haunted. Some, however, seem to be, and ghost hunters regularly investigate them. The Whaley House in San Diego is said to be among the most paranormally active in the United States. If this one is not in your zip code, paranormal experts in your area will know of local houses with haunted reputations. (To find these experts in your area, use a search engine such as Google. Use keywords "ghost hunter," "paranormal investigations," and the names of your city and state.)

San Diego's Whaley House is called one of the most haunted houses in America. Members of the Whaley family and hanging victim Yankee Jim are said to wander its halls.

People have captured residual ghostly images in the Whaley House theater. Furniture once used onstage appeared in a photo—even though it was packed in a storeroom down the hall. Ghosts of the Whaley family and Yankee Jim, a thief hanged in 1857 on the Whaley property before the house was built, are all said to haunt this home.

Some claim that a cat and a dog haunt the Whaley House too. A tour guide told me about a skeptic who had challenged the story of the pet dog's ghost making friendly contact. The man dropped to his hands and knees to prove his point, beckoning the dog from under the master's bed, saying, "Come on, doggy. Come on and lick me on the nose."

Suddenly, he leapt to his feet, his face pale. The guide asked him what happened. He said he'd felt the spirit dog's wet tongue do exactly what he'd asked.

HOTELS

Hotels are homes away from home for many people. Some travel to their favorite destinations for restful vacations. Some celebrate special occasions such as weddings, birthdays, or anniversaries at their favorite hotel. That strong sense of connection may be responsible for the fact that many hotels are thought to be

Lisa Yee's Real-Life Haunted House Story

Lisa Yee is known for her funny middle-grade fiction. But during a stay at the Thurber House, things got weird. When she heard about this book, she offered to tell me what happened. Here's her story:

"Are you scared of ghosts?" asked the woman calling from the Thurber House in Columbus, Ohio.

"No," I told her, "I don't believe in ghosts."

As any sane person knows, ghosts are figments of overactive imaginations, poofs of dust or smoke that inflict themselves on clueless people in movies who stumble into creepy mansions after midnight.

When I was selected to be the Thurber House's children's writer-in-residence, I got to live in James Thurber's home for four weeks. One of the twentieth century's most popular humorists, Thurber spent part of his young adulthood in the house. The historic Victorian residence was built on the site of the Ohio Lunatic Asylum. In 1868 a fire destroyed the asylum, trapping and killing several residents.

On my first night in the private attic apartment that housed the writers-in-residence, I nosed through the dresser drawers. I discovered a list of paranormal activities previous writers-in-residence had experienced and written about. Some had seen the shadow of a man on the wall, others had felt his presence, and a few had witnessed books flying off the shelves.

All alone at night, I'd hear footsteps, just as James Thurber had reported. He wrote "The Night the Ghost Got In," a short story about his ghostly encounter, which occurred exactly forty-seven years after the insane asylum had burned down.

It was kind of quaint, I mused. A house ghost. Of course, I knew there really was no such thing. Oh, sure, bolted windows flew open on their own and lightbulbs flickered at odd hours. Okay, so the radio changed channels when no one was near. And, yes, my computer acted up, but it always did that.

Before I knew it, four weeks had passed. On my last day, I awoke at 4:45 a.m. and made my way downstairs to wait for my ride to the airport. It was still dark, but I didn't bother with the lights. By then I knew the house backward and forward. However, as I attempted to pass through the dining room doorway, something stopped me. When I pushed to get through, it pushed back. It felt like the force between two opposing magnets. Or like I was swimming. Or like a wall of Jell-O. It defied logic. Maybe, I thought, I had stumbled into a massive spiderweb.

When I turned on the lights, nothing was there. I was confused, but I wasn't scared. A feeling of calm washed over me. I knew what had just happened.

"You're real, aren't you?" I said out loud.

I'm still not sure if I believe in ghosts. But I do believe this—during all those weeks living in the attic apartment of Thurber House, I was not alone.

haunted. If someone loved a hotel and died there, returning to haunt that place seems possible.

The Stanley Hotel in Estes Park, Colorado, is one of the most famous haunted hotels in the United States. The site is more than one hundred years old. Freelan Stanley and his wife, Flora, had it built in 1907 to take advantage of the region's healthy environment (He had bouts of tuberculosis).

When the hauntings began is uncertain, but reports of seeing the ghost of housekeeper Elizabeth Wilson folding clothes date back to the 1950s. Nearly every room at the Stanley has exhibited paranormal activity, including lights turning on and off on their own, belongings being packed and unpacked, disembodied voices and laughter, and the sound of piano music from Flora's beloved music room.

Colorado's Stanley Hotel inspired horror writer Stephen King to write *The Shining*.

Because of this activity, the Stanley Hotel employs a full-time psychic (a person who can "read" people and "see" their past, present, and future), Madame Vera, as well as a paranormal investigator, Lisa Nyhart, to lead ghostly tours.

Some television investigators claim angry ghosts wander the halls of the Stanley. The people who work at the hotel disagree. They insist their ghosts are friendly spirits of former employees or guests, including Lucy, Paul, Eddie, and

Do spirits walk the halls of the Stanley Hotel? Many former guests believe they do.

Elizabeth. They admit Eddie sometimes haunts with a foul odor—but, they add, so do some of their living guests.

"We have more nights with activity than without," Nyhart says of the Stanley. "It's a Disneyland for spirits."

The Stanley's huge halls and otherworldly inhabitants have inspired some people. On October 30, 1974, novelist Stephen King and his wife Tabitha were the only two guests at the hotel, inspiring one of his scariest books, *The Shining*.

MORE EVIDENCE: THE DAVENPORT HOTEL

Some visitors of this restored, turn-of-the-twentieth-century luxury hotel in Spokane, Washington, say it is haunted by Louis and Verus Davenport, the couple who had it built. Before Louis died, he swore he would never leave the hotel, and many employees are convinced he followed through on his words. But its most famous ghost is Ellen McNamara.

McNamara fell to her death through a Tiffany skylight on August 17, 1920. She crashed to the marble floors below and died in her hotel room several hours later, whispering, "Where did I go? Where did I go?"

People have claimed to have heard those words whispered in the same lobby. Some have seen an apparition of McNamara dressed in a 1920s flapper dress as well. Other ghosts have pushed luggage carts, thrown open heavy doors, and even danced in the hotel ballrooms.

Skeptics say the vivid, well-documented history of the hotel sparks the imaginations of guests and employees when natural explanations make more sense: The wind moves the heavy doors. And tilted floors make the carts move without human force.

Hotel representative Tom McArthur tries to stay neutral. "As an official spokesperson of the hotel, I can never say, 'We have ghosts or don't have ghosts,'" he explains in the *Pacific Northwest Inlander* newspaper. "But based on what enough people have told me, we might."

BATTLEFIELDS

Some people believe battlefields are often haunted. They were the sites of bloody clashes that led to many deaths. Some believers think haunting can take on a visible form.

As mentioned earlier, the Civil War's bloodiest battle took place at Gettysburg, Pennsylvania. For months, fields around the town of Gettysburg served as temporary graveyards. Many homes, churches, and other buildings became hospitals for more than twenty thousand wounded. Not surprisingly, paranormal investigators search for ghostly activity in this area.

For more than one hundred years, witnesses have claimed to see and hear what they believe are spirits of Gettysburg soldiers. Some have seen residual images of ghostly armies waging battle. Others have heard moans and screams. Some have even seen ghosts of Civil War animals.

One of the most compelling stories took place during the filming of the 1993 blockbuster motion picture *Gettysburg.* Reenactors and local residents were cast as extras, most as soldiers in the battle scenes.

While some extras were taking a break—still in their Union army uniforms— on the rocky ground of Little Round Top, they met a tattered old soldier who smelled of sulfury gunpowder. "Rough one today, eh, boys?" he whispered as they crossed paths. Then he handed the actors three musket balls and walked on. When they showed the metal balls to the film's prop manager, he said they weren't his reproductions. The ammunition turned out to be authentic musket balls, roughly 130 years old at the time. No one could explain the mystery.

Thousands of soldiers from both the North and the South died at Gettysburg, Pennsylvania, during the Civil War. Some people say the soldiers' spirits can still be felt, seen, and heard on the battlefields.

Do ghosts haunt Gettysburg? It's hard to be sure these moments aren't purely imaginary. But even Union army hero Joshua Chamberlain suggested it was possible. When monuments to his regiment, the Twentieth Maine, were dedicated on October 3, 1889, he said, "On great fields, something remains. Forms change and pass; bodies disappear; but spirits linger, to consecrate ground for the vision-place of souls. And reverent men and women from afar, and generations that know us not and that we know not of, . . . shall come to this deathless field, to ponder and dream; and lo! the shadow of a mighty presence shall wrap them in its bosom, and the power of the vision pass into their souls."

MORE EVIDENCE: THE ALAMO

The site of the battle of the Alamo, in San Antonio, Texas, is one of the most haunted battle sites in the state. In 1836 Mexican general Antonio López de Santa Anna and his 4,000-man army defeated 189 rebellious Texans, including Jim Bowie and Davy Crockett. Reports of paranormal activity began after the battle, when Sam Houston and his men captured Santa Anna. Santa Anna sent word to his troops to burn the Alamo to the ground. But according to some accounts, when his torch-bearing men approached the old fortress, six apparitions allegedly appeared, saying, "Do not touch the Alamo. Do not touch these walls." The soldiers fled in fear.

A second group of Mexican troops went to finish the mission. They retreated after a single apparition holding a blazing fireball in each hand allegedly appeared on the roof. For the next ten years, the Mexican Army refused to go near the infamous Alamo.

The ghostly activity continued in the late nineteenth century when San Antonio police tried to use the old fortress as a station and jail. Almost immediately, inmates complained that the jail was haunted. Reports of disembodied moans, shuffling sounds, and ghosts standing guard on the Alamo roof were common.

Some believe the haunting continues today. People say they have seen soldiers on the roof of the popular tourist attraction. Some have described a rain-drenched cowboy. Others have reported seeing a little boy searching for his father, who died in the battle. Even the spirit of Davy Crockett has allegedly been seen, complete with buckskin clothing and a coonskin cap.

GRAVEYARDS

Bachelor's Grove Cemetery near Chicago, Illinois, has a colorful, crime-linked past. Gangster Al Capone moved to Chicago from New York City in the 1920s. Cemetery folklore says when Capone "took out" his enemies, he dumped their bodies in the Bachelor's Grove Cemetery pond. Their spirits allegedly haunt the place. But Capone's enemies aren't the only ghosts at the cemetery.

One of the best-known photographs of an apparition ever captured was taken at Bachelor's Grove Cemetery. She has become known as the White Lady. Shot in black and white by Judy Felz on August 10, 1991, the image features a long-haired, transparent woman in a flowing white dress, sitting on a checkerboard grave marker, her feet and face a blur.

"The first time I went through my stack of photos, I didn't see anything," Felz says in a Travel Channel documentary. "The second time, I happened to see this lady sitting on the headstone, and I almost jumped through the ceiling." Felz believes she has captured a full-fledged apparition. But Midwest Haunts investigator Jason Sullivan says it's a fake.

"The picture has incredible detail and [the figure] casts a shadow, which tells me light couldn't past through it. It must be solid," he says. Sullivan believes his

Do apparitions haunt the graves in Bachelor's Grove near Chicago, Illinois? Paranormal investigators think they might.

own 2004 Bachelor's Grove apparition photo is more authentic. "I still stare at it to this day," he says. Because the female ghost was standing near a marked grave, Sullivan calls her by the name on that marker—the Lady of the Grove Dora Newman.

MORE EVIDENCE: HOWARD STREET CEMETERY

If you think ghosts are scary, try a combination of ghosts and witches. At Howard Street Cemetery in historic Salem, Massachusetts, the stories of real-life tragedy sometimes mix with eerie events.

In September 1692, four young girls—Mercy Lewis, Ann Putnam Jr., Abigail Williams, and Mary Wolcott—accused seventy-one-year-old Giles Corey and his wife, Martha, of witchcraft. Because he refused to be tried in a court he felt had already judged him as guilty, Corey received an especially cruel punishment. The old man was stripped of his clothes; lowered on his back into a pit at the Howard Street Cemetery, just outside the Salem jailhouse; and "pressed." Planks of wood were placed on his bare skin and heavy stones were added, one by one by one. With each stone, Judge Samuel Sewall asked Corey to confess, but he refused again and again, saying only, "More weight!"

Giles Corey was the only accused who was "pressed to death" as a result of the Salem witch trials in Salem, Massachusetts, in 1692. Nineteen others were hanged, and several died in jail awaiting trial.

After two days, Corey passed away and was buried in an unmarked grave in the Howard Street Cemetery. Martha was hanged on Gallows Hill on September 22. She was among the last of those executed for witchcraft.

The Coreys and other victims of the Salem witch trials were laid to rest in Howard Street Cemetery, one of the oldest graveyards in New England. A marker has since been erected in memory of Giles Corey. According to local ghost hunter Joann Hoxha, his angry spirit haunts the cemetery. She says he appears as a ghostly orb in photographs, and she senses an uneasy chill on the grounds. She's even captured electronic voice evidence of him screaming, "Get out!"

PRISONS

In decades past, prisons were dark, dangerous places—holding tanks for criminals and the mentally ill alike. Were all the prisoners who died in these places actually guilty of a crime? Not necessarily. Certainly, some inmates were guilty. They could have died filled with anger. But what about the rage of the innocent? Either way, some may have had good reasons to feel eternally connected to their prisons.

The Old Idaho Penitentiary in Boise, Idaho, is no exception. Opened in 1872 as a single cellblock, it was home to eleven of the Idaho Territory's vilest criminals. By the time it closed in 1973, the prison had grown into a giant fortress of stone, built by prisoners confined there. During the summer, the cells baked, often reaching 120°F (49°C) inside. In winter, temperatures dropped to well below freezing.

During the century it was open, more than 13,000 inmates—including 222 women—served their sentences. Some were put to death. The first 6 killed dangled from the gallows in the prison yard. When executions were scheduled, families from Boise packed picnic lunches and hiked into the hills surrounding the high prison walls to watch. Later, the prison moved the gallows inside, to Section Five, where, in modern times, visitors reportedly have heard and seen ghostly screams and shadow figures.

Some preferred to choose their own fate. Douglas Van Vlack, prisoner 5264, was sentenced to hang in December 1937, for killing his wife, but he never made it to the gallows. After visiting his mother, Van Vlack slipped past the prison guards and climbed to the rafters above the cellblock.

"My mother told me it was all right for me to choose the way I wanted to die. I'll never hang on that rope." Those were Van Vlack's last words before he dove headfirst onto the concrete floor. He died instantly. Tour guides say his spirit still wanders the cellblock where he died.

Another murderer, Idaho's "Jack the Ripper," Raymond Snowden, is the ghost most often sighted at the Idaho prison. The court convicted Snowden of murdering his girlfriend Cora Dean—slashing her throat and snapping her spine at the base of her skull—in September 1956. Snowden showed no remorse. He bragged about his crime and confessed to another killing before he was hanged in 1957. Most death row convicts had died within seconds of dropping through the gallows floor, but Snowden lingered a full fifteen minutes, as if refusing to meet his maker.

Paranormal investigators, including the Travel Channel's *Ghost Adventures* team, have collected evidence of the killer's ghost haunting the gallows. They have claimed Snowden grabbed their arms and revealed himself as a dark shadow figure. Photographic evidence has been sketchy, but uneasy feelings among the building's visitors seem universal.

MORE EVIDENCE:
EASTERN STATE PENITENTIARY

While you may never see the inside of a modern prison, exploring a haunted former prison might be an experience you'll never forget. Dozens of retired penitentiaries are open to tourists and ghost hunters. Ghostly investigations may take place at a prison near you, especially around Halloween.

In 1787 Benjamin Franklin joined with the Philadelphia Society for Alleviating the Miseries of Public Prisons to create a new system of punishment. Making criminals pay for their crimes was the primary focus of the new Eastern State Penitentiary in Philadelphia, but religious repentance for sins was another goal. Society members hoped solitary confinement of guilty prisoners would help them accept their punishment, repent, and go on to live better lives.

Prisoners in solitary confinement had no family visits and no news from outside the prison walls. The only human contact was the delivery of meals by prison guards. Five years after it opened, the prison was investigated for claims

Prisoners experienced extremely harsh treatment at Eastern State Penitentiary. Some witnesses claim the ghosts of dead inmates still haunt this abandoned prison.

of inmate abuse. One sixteen-year-old boy was punished for cutting shoe leather. He spent forty-two days in a tiny dirt-floored punishment cell with no food and no light. Investigators found him starving to death and temporarily insane. Another young prisoner, a nineteen-year-old, was stripped to the waist and forced by prison guards to take a brutal cold-water bath outdoors in the icy Pennsylvania winter, though no reason was documented. Inmates who were caught trying to talk with fellow prisoners wore "the iron gag," a 5-inch (13 cm) piece of metal that held the tongue and wrapped around the head and was connected by a chain to handcuffs behind the prisoner's back. At least one prisoner did not survive this torture.

Ghostly activity allegedly began in the 1940s, thirty years before the prison closed. Witnesses have described mysterious knocks on the pipes from lonely souls in search of human contact, cries in the night, ghostly shadows, and apparitions—even more so after the building was retired in 1971. Paranormal investigators continue to visit the prison, which is now preserved as a historic place. They still search for proof that some of the inmates never left—and try to help some souls move on.

SHIPS

Not all haunted places are stationary and on land. People who make the sea their life's work—fishermen, sailors, and ships' crews—know they can sail for years or even decades. Sometimes, these people pass away while aboard. With such intense personal connections, it's not surprising that some vessels are thought to be haunted.

One ship with ample cause to be haunted is the USS *Arizona*. On the morning of December 7, 1941, just before 8:00 a.m., bomber planes from the Imperial

The USS *Arizona* was launched in 1915 and sank during the 1941 attack on Pearl Harbor.

Japanese Navy rocketed over the battleship and her sister ships docked in Pearl Harbor, Hawaii. By 8:06 a.m., four bombs had ripped through the steel of the USS *Arizona,* sending her to a watery grave in Pearl Harbor. And 1,177 of the ship's 1,512 crewmen died with her.

Authorities never recovered the USS *Arizona* and her victims. The Pacific War Memorial Commission built a memorial above the shipwreck to honor the men who were lost.

Is the USS *Arizona* haunted by the men who served on board? Many memorial visitors have said it is. They claimed that faces of young soldiers often appear on the surface of the water surrounding the memorial. Some have said they heard whispers from the attack's victims.

MORE EVIDENCE: THE *DELTA KING*

Built in the 1920s, the *Delta King* is an old-fashioned riverboat, complete with a working paddle wheel. It cruised the Sacramento River in California for twenty years, traveling from Sacramento to San Francisco. During World War II, it transported soldiers. After the boat sank in 1982, the future of the *Delta King* looked bleak. But a businessman bought and restored it as a floating hotel in Sacramento in 1984.

Sacramento's *Delta King* may be haunted by a young girl who likes to sing to hotel guests.

Guests have claimed several ghosts haunt the riverboat. These apparitions have included a restless old man in a tattered hat who wanders through the lobby as though he's lost or searching for something. The star spirit is a nine-year-old girl.

Witnesses, including guests and staff members, have said a blond girl in a long, white dress skipped down the outdoor hallways, giggling and leaving wet footprints. She has been known to bounce a rubber ball and sing the song, "Ring around the Rosy." Only male witnesses have seen the girl's apparition. She is the ghost reported most frequently.

Some people say she was murdered on the *Delta King*. Others say she died a natural death and lingers because the boat was a place she loved. No documentation exists to prove either theory.

The only other ghostly activity at the *Delta King* is the frequent, unexplained shattering of water glasses. They seem to tip and fall suddenly and without cause in the riverboat's dining areas. The boat is docked on the waters of the Sacramento River and was built to deflect the rolling motion of the water, causing it to tilt slightly. That soft sloping could explain the breaking glasses—but not the playful ghost of a little girl.

CHAPTER THREE

GHOST HUNTERS

Throughout history, a select group of people have claimed to have a direct connection with the dead. Long ago, religious scholars explored otherworldly matters. Scientific thinkers of their day often disagreed with them. Today many paranormal investigators embrace science and use a variety of tools in an effort to find solid evidence to prove ghosts are real—or to prove they're not.

RELIGIOUS SCHOLARS OF THE PAST

Joseph Glanvill

Joseph Glanvill was a spiritual adviser to King Charles II in seventeenth-century England. He was known as a religious scholar. Glanvill wrote on many subjects, but he primarily focused on witchcraft and ghosts.

Glanvill was sure ghosts and witches were real. Many challenged his theories on ghosts, but Glanvill clung to his beliefs. He thought the existence of ghosts proved the existence of God.

Glanvill cited passages in the Bible as evidence that ghosts were real. He called denial of their existence a step away from God. Although he died in 1680, Glanvill's book *Saducismus Triumphatus or Full and Plain Evidence concerning Witches and Apparitions* was published in 1681. The book confirmed the existence of witches for many and influenced judges like Cotton Mather to sentence men and women to death during the Salem witch trials in Massachusetts.

Glanvill offered some powerful stories but did little to actually prove anything paranormal. In one example, Glanvill wrote about a woman killed with a pickax by a man who hid her body in the depths of a coalpit. According to Glanvill, she rose as a bloody apparition to expose her killer in an act of afterlife revenge.

Christoph Friedrich Nicolai

Christoph Friedrich Nicolai was a German bookseller, a scholar, and a philosopher. He was so devoted to his books that he came down with a case of "violent giddiness," according to his doctors. Twice a year, they bled him with leeches to control the symptoms. After he missed a treatment in 1790, Nicolai began to see ghosts.

Nicolai thought his visions might be caused by the missed bleeding, but he didn't seek medical help. He wondered, instead, what he could learn about the apparitions by prolonging his illness. He decided to put off any treatments so he could find out.

Nicolai observed his ghostly visitors for months, describing his experiences in writing. Dozens of spirits swirled around him, according to his journals, although his wife never saw one. He didn't let his odd condition worry him—at least not until the ghosts started talking to him. That, he thought, was too much. He sought out his doctors and their thirsty leeches, and then turned his journals into a report.

In 1799 Nicolai presented his observations to a group of German scientists called the Royal Society of Berlin. He titled his paper "A Memoir on the Appearance of Spectres or Phantoms Occasioned by Disease, with Psychological Remarks." When it was translated into English in 1803, Nicolai's report forever changed the way British scholars looked at people who claimed to see ghosts. Those who read his books no longer thought people who saw ghosts were being visited by spirits. Instead, they thought these people were crazy.

Later, Nicolai set himself apart from people he called "insane," "fanatical," "superstitious," and "lovers of the marvelous," saying he never really believed the ghosts were real. Our eyes can deceive us, he concluded, so we should consider ghostly visions as being haunted by our own imaginations.

POPULAR MODERN INVESTIGATORS
Jason Hawes

The scientific study of ghosts took a giant step forward in October 2004, when SyFy launched the television series *Ghost Hunters*. Jason Hawes led TAPS (The Atlantic Paranormal Society) team members as they investigated claims of paranormal activity. More and more viewers tuned in, and people started taking the topic more seriously. Ten years later, the show is still popular.

Other paranormal investigation groups existed long before TAPS and *Ghost Hunters,* but Hawes is unique in that his primary goal is not to scare but to gather information. His team actively debunks (disproves) ghostly evidence whenever possible. The group's willingness to admit most things are not of paranormal origins gives the show and the team greater credibility. When the *Ghost Hunters* team discovers evidence they cannot debunk, its paranormal possibility becomes more powerful. Viewers feel they can trust the team to tell the truth, whatever that truth turns out to be. TAPS team members almost always reassure their clients that they are in no physical danger, even if the activity they are experiencing could be otherworldly.

Some critics, including Joe Nickell at the *Skeptical Inquirer,* say the science TAPS members use is sketchy, some evidence is faked, and the show encourages superstitious beliefs. However, Hawes denies the accusations. He insists everything shown on *Ghost Hunters* is real and the team's credibility has contributed to the show's survival.

From left to right: the cast from *Ghost Hunters* season 9 includes Samantha Hawes, Dave Tango, Jason Hawes, Adam Berry, Steve Gonsalves, Britt Griffith, and Amy Bruni.

What do paranormal investigators use to scare up evidence of ghosts? Let's take a look at what you'll find in a typical ghost-hunter's toolbox.

1) DIGITAL CAMERA. A digital camera is an important piece of ghost-hunting equipment. A camera may pick up evidence the eyes can't detect.

2) DIGITAL RECORDER. Paranormal investigators use digital recorders to search for electronic voice phenomena (mysterious voices or sounds picked up by digital recorders). The idea is that spirits, as forces of electrical energy, can speak through recorders on frequencies our ears can't hear.

3) DIGITAL THERMOMETER. Many investigators carry a digital thermometer to document any sudden drop in temperatures, known as cold spots. Ghost hunters say such drops accompany the presence of a ghostly energy.

4) DOWSING RODS. For centuries, people used two L-shaped branches to search for water underground. If the two branches crossed over each other as the person holding them walked, it meant water was under the person's feet. If the branches didn't cross, the person should keep walking. Paranormal investigators use L-shaped rods made of copper to ask ghostly visitors questions. If the rods cross, the answer is yes. If the rods remain apart, the answer is no. Because there is no way to prove the person holding the rods isn't causing them to cross, the practice is considered unreliable.

5) EMF METER. Electromagnetic field (EMF) indicators weren't originally made for hunting ghosts. They were made for electricians. Electrical wiring often creates an electromagnetic field. When there is too much electromagnetism in an area, people can experience a creepy-crawly sensation on their skin. Paranormal experts say it can also cause dizziness and confusion. Those responses can also be due to paranormal activity, so an EMF meter comes in handy to help tell the difference. But ghost hunters say it's also possible for ghostly entities to communicate by lighting up the meter's tiny, colorful bulbs.

6) FLASHLIGHT. As simple as it sounds, ghostly entities reportedly can cause an ordinary flashlight to flicker to answer yes-or-no questions.

7) MOTION SENSOR (NOT SHOWN). By projecting a tiny beam of light across a hallway or a room, a motion sensor can alert investigators when something breaks the beam, including a ghost. An alarm sounds and lights flash, so the investigators know where to go to interact with that particular spirit.

8) OVILUS SPIRIT BOX (NOT SHOWN). If ghosts can trigger electronic devices, paranormal investigators believe spirits can also trigger the Ovilus, a device created to produce more than two thousand preprogrammed words. Ghost hunters believe when a spirit is close to the box, the spirit can trigger the box to say a word the spirit wants to communicate.

9) VIDEO CAMERA (NOT SHOWN). Video cameras equipped with night-vision lenses may capture shadow figures, apparitions, mist, and orbs in real time for more careful analysis after the investigation has concluded. Debunking video evidence is easier once you have finished the investigation and review the film later.

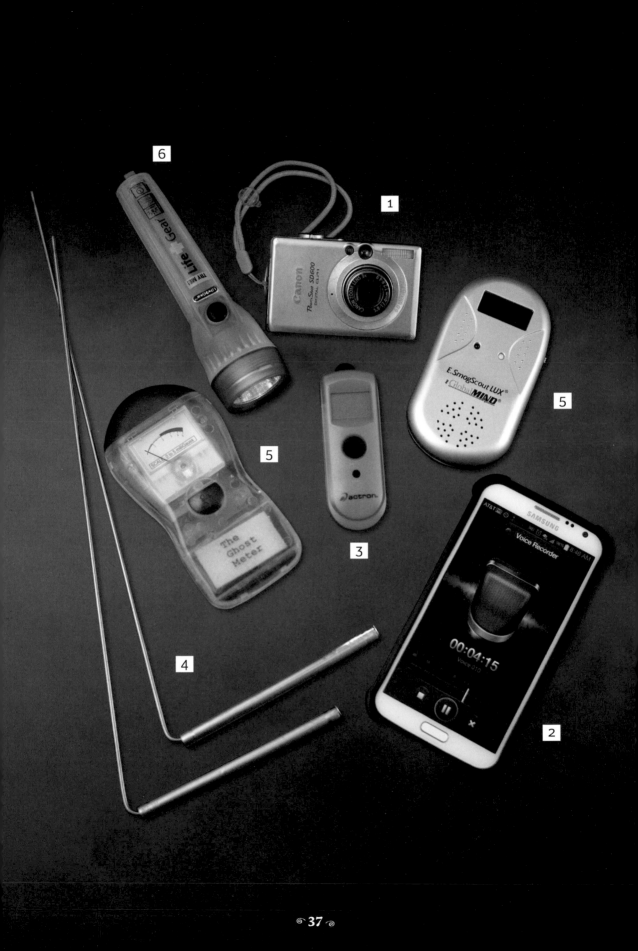

Zak Bagans

While friendly spirits are more typical on *Ghost Hunters,* Zak Bagans and the team at *Ghost Adventures* seem to attract energy from the opposite end of the ghostly spectrum. The Travel Channel series, starring Bagans and his crew, embraces the drama of angry ghosts. This sets their show apart from *Ghost Hunters.*

Bagans's interest in the paranormal began when he allegedly came face-to-face with a female ghost at his apartment in Flint, Michigan. According to the series introduction, Bagans hopes to capture something similar on film.

Best known for his confrontational approach to communicating with the dead, Bagans often badgers and challenges the spirit energies to do him physical harm, especially when he investigates prisons, abandoned mental institutions, or other rough environments. It's an approach some consider disrespectful and counterproductive. Unlike TAPS, Bagans says demons—rather than ghosts—sometimes frequent the haunted locales he visits. He enlisted the help of a Catholic priest to exorcise one of these entities that he felt had attached itself to him. Even so, Bagans claims to avoid any religious connections in his investigations.

Bagans and his team debunk some of their videotaped evidence, on and off camera, but the show's primary focus is on what ghostly evidence they *might* have captured on film.

Celebrity ghost hunter Zak Bagans lead investigator on *Ghost Adventures,* examines a Mel meter (a type of EMF meter) as he points into an old opium den in the Shanghai Tunnels in Portland, Oregon.

Alane Ferguson, Paranormal Investigator and Writer

Writer Alane Ferguson has published more than thirty novels, many of which feature otherworldly spirits. Inspired by *Ghost Hunters* episodes, she set out to collect evidence of her own.

"In one of the first episodes," she said, "a chair moved in an abandoned building's attic, and I thought, 'This is either real evidence of paranormal activity, or somebody is using a fishing line and pulling the chair to get a reaction from the audience.' I decided the only way to know for sure was to try ghost hunting myself."

She has collected evidence to suggest that spirits try to communicate through electronic tools. "The most effective piece of equipment I have found is my EMF [electromagnetic field] meter. There are five lights, ranging from green to red, on the end of the meter," she explained. An EMF meter works like this: the green light stays lit the whole time the meter is on, but the others light up to indicate an increase in an area's electromagnetic field. "It takes a *lot* to get them to light up, so when those tiny bulbs go off, it's like watching fingers running up and down piano keys," Ferguson continued. "When it goes all the way to red, I know something's cooking!

"In addition, I have an image of a ghost walking in front of my infrared camera in a haunted room in Ault, Colorado. I could go on and on, but after reviewing all my evidence, I have come to the conclusion that spirits walk among us!"

Ferguson is convinced, but she's not afraid. "Ghosts do not scare me, because I think they are just people. Most go into the light to find peace. But ghosts with 'unfinished business' can be trapped here as earthbound spirits. If I sense there is someone like that who is trying to communicate with me, I will tell them to go into the light and be happy."

For anyone frightened by ghosts that haunt them, Ferguson has some advice: "A spirit cannot stay if it is not welcome, so ask the cranky ghost to leave. But if you're comfortable with a friendly spirit, enjoy the fact that someone cares for you, and try not to be scared. Ghosts were people, too!"

Theresa Caputo

Theresa Caputo, the namesake of TLC's *Long Island Medium,* grew up in Hicksville, New York. Nothing seemed out of the ordinary about her until Caputo turned four. Out of nowhere, a tattered apparition she called a hobo started haunting her wherever she went.

She explained in her autobiography, *There Is More to Life Than This,* that he later became one of her spiritual guides. But when she was a child, this hobo ghost frightened her. The sight of her hobo was so unsettling that she almost never left her home, except to go to school.

Caputo began to wonder why other people didn't see what she saw or hear the voices she heard. At sixteen, she began to understand. Others didn't see and hear them because her "visitors" weren't alive. They were coming to her from the other side.

Confirmation came after her grandmother passed away. Caputo could still see her and once talked to her as her cousins watched. "Theresa, who are you talking to?" they asked her. She answered, "I'm talking to Nanny," the nickname her grandmother used.

"She's dead," they said, laughing at what they thought was a joke. Caputo told them she knew that, but it didn't stop Nanny from talking. At that moment, the young girl realized she had a spiritual gift.

Confiding in her teenage friends didn't go well. "That's when my trouble all started. When I started sharing with my friends, and they'd say, 'Well, that's not normal,' and then I shut down."

Caputo tried to be "normal," to ignore the conversations, until a spiritual adviser helped her learn how to manage the talents. She had to learn how to shut out the voices when she needed time to herself and how to help them when she was willing to help. Today, Caputo shares messageswith the living from people who have passed on. She does it on television, while grocery shopping, wherever she goes. She has committed her life to helping grieving people connect with loved ones they've lost, and it's a full-time job.

"They just want us to know they are okay, especially when someone passes in a tragedy," she says. "They want to make their presence known, to say they are at peace."

CHAPTER FOUR

SUPERNATURAL HOAXES

Many twenty-first-century paranormal investigators are sincere in their efforts to collect ghostly evidence, but this hasn't always been the case. After the Civil War and World War I, phony performers saw the grief-stricken as piggy banks. If these con artists could convince the grieving to pay for the special skills they offered—the ability to talk with or photograph the dead—they'd be rich and famous.

Dozens of these deceivers roamed the world making remarkable claims. Most were eventually found out, but not before they had robbed numerous people. This chapter explores just a few of these charlatans—and exposes how some hoaxes are created.

KATIE AND MAGGIE FOX, DECEPTIVE SISTERS

In 1848 eleven-year-old Katie Fox and her fifteen-year-old sister, Maggie, told their neighbor that ghosts were knocking on the walls of their Hydesville, New York, home. The neighbor, Mary Redfield, thought the girls were playing a childish prank until their panicked father appeared at Redfield's door asking for help too. Those knocks marked the birth of a movement called modern spiritualism in the United States. Ghosts—and the mediums who could make contact with them—became wildly popular in the nineteenth century.

This daguerrotype, taken in 1852. shows Katie *(left)* and Maggie Fox *(right)*, the two sisters who claimed they could communicate with the dead.

The Fox sisters claimed they had a connection to spirits in the afterlife, and people listened. Their older, married sister, Leah Underhill, saw money in her younger sisters' gift, so she became their manager, and the trio went on the road. Moving from city to city and stage to stage, they filled huge auditoriums, promising to communicate with the dead through otherworldly knocks. Time after time, the paying crowds were not disappointed. The Fox sisters were a hit.

Famous people, including author James Fenimore Cooper, sought out the girls. Cooper hosted a private audience and became a devout believer. His sister had died in a horseback-riding accident, and he never got over the loss. He tested the sisters, asking when he'd lost his closest loved one. The spirits slowly knocked thirty-eight times—the exact number of years since Cooper's sister had passed away. It was a fact, he said, the sisters could not have known.

For decades, the girls reigned as top spiritual guides, until Maggie made a startling confession to reporters at the *New York World* newspaper in October 1888. "We discovered a new way to make raps," Maggie admitted. "Katie was the first to observe that by swishing her fingers, she could produce certain noises with her knuckles and joints, and that the same effect could be made with the toes. We practiced until we could do this easily when the room was dark . . . . Many people when they hear the rapping imagine at once the spirits are touching them," she continued. "It is a very common delusion."

Maggie later retracted her confession, saying she was paid $1,500 to make it. She said she wanted to hurt Leah, whom she felt had been unkind to her and Katie. But she had shattered the public's trust.

WILLIAM H. MUMLER, SPIRIT PHOTOGRAPHER

During the Civil War, more than six hundred thousand Confederate and Union soldiers died or were killed, leaving their loved ones grieving and aching for a sign, some evidence that these people weren't forever gone. Photographer William H. Mumler tried to give those who survived the tragic loss of their soldiers comforting evidence through his spirit photographs. One of his first doctored prints was a self-portrait. His photo was clear and clean, but just over his shoulder was the image of his cousin, who had died twelve years before the photograph was made. He made the photo by simply taking two photos on one plate, something known as double exposure.

Mumler used a double-exposure method to add the "ghost" of Abraham Lincoln standing behind Lincoln's widow, Mary Todd Lincoln, seen sitting here.

Over time, Mumler's photographs grew enormously popular. One of the most compelling photos, taken in 1871, showed the living widow and former first lady Mary Todd Lincoln with the apparition of President Abraham Lincoln standing behind her, six years after his assassination. A grieving nation paid attention. Spiritualists and the lonely flocked to Mumler's studios in Boston, Massachusetts, and New York, New York, hoping to claim a ghostly image of their own.

One of Mumler's customers was P. T. Barnum. The famed showman purchased several of Mumler's photographs for "A Proof of Humbugs," a traveling exhibition of items produced to fool the public. When Mumler was sued for selling falsified photographs in 1869, Barnum testified against him. The judge scolded Mumler for what he believed were deceptive images.

However, he admitted that the prosecution had not produced enough hard evidence to prove its case. Mumler was found not guilty and claimed victory. Even so, his career as a ghost photographer was over.

HARRY HOUDINI, FRAUD DETECTOR

Most people know Harry Houdini, an American immigrant from Budapest, Hungary, as a magician and death-defying escape artist. By freeing himself from handcuffs, straitjackets, and locked tanks of water, Houdini dazzled audiences around the world. He even pretended to be a medium in his early years as a performer.

When his beloved mother, Cecilia Weisz, died in 1913, Houdini was devastated. He spent hours lying on her grave, wishing he could speak to her just one more time. He knew his medium act was an illusion, but he wondered if some mediums might be real. He mounted a quest—to find one spiritualist with a genuine gift.

To Houdini's dismay, the quest was unsuccessful. His background allowed him to easily spot and expose hoaxes. In 1923 he toured the United States lecturing about fraudulent mediums and wrote a book called *A Magician among the Spirits,* published a year later. He joined *Scientific American* magazine in offering a reward for any mediums who could prove their gifts were authentic.

Mina Crandon, also known as Margery, came forward to claim the prize. Houdini's close friend, Britain's Sir Arthur Conan Doyle (author of the Sherlock

Harry Houdini *(right)*, J. Malcolm Bird *(top)*, and O. D. Munn *(left)* were all members of the committee that investigated the famous medium Mina Crandon *(center)*, a.k.a. Margery, during her Boston séances. Houdini never believed she could actually communicate with ghosts.

Holmes stories), believed Crandon was beyond reproach. But the skeptical Houdini could not agree. "I've got her," Houdini said after watching her perform a séance. He publicly declared her work "all fraud." The committee was divided about awarding her the prize, so it was never given. Houdini's friendship with Doyle ended because of the disagreement. But Doyle and many of Margery's other followers continued to defend her.

Before Houdini died at the age of fifty-two in 1926, he shared a secret code with his wife, Bess. He promised his beloved wife he would find a way to contact her from the afterlife. Revealing the secret code would be proof that his spirit was communicating with her. After he died, Bess continued his work of exposing fraudulent mediums. But she also hoped to hear from her husband.

Each year, Bess hosted a séance, offering $10,000 to any medium who could produce the code passed from husband to wife. Houdini's widow gave up on Halloween 1936, saying, "Ten years is long enough to wait for any man."

HELEN DUNCAN, FABRICATOR OF SPIRITS

In most ways, Helen Duncan was an ordinary Scottish wife and mother of nine. However, she did claim to have some spiritual gifts—vague feelings she called psychic—but nothing that caused a stir. Then, in 1926, out of the blue, she announced she was a medium. As she began holding séances for paying customers, Duncan drew attention, first from believers and later from skeptics.

Duncan claimed she could produce physical proof of the dearly departed. Visible apparitions floated through the air as she slipped into a trance. However, her reputation took a hit in 1928 when photographer Harvey Metcalfe took flash photographs during a séance. The photographs brought Duncan's "ghosts" into focus, exposing doll-face masks, white fabric bodies, and coat-hanger shoulders dangling from strings.

Eventually, Duncan claimed to produce ectoplasm (supernatural matter made by mediums' bodies to allow spirits to take a physical form). In other words, a medium somehow produced a material that ghosts supposedly used to become visible. Other mediums had been caught with fake ectoplasm during Duncan's heyday. Some sewed false pockets into their dresses and pulled the material from their clothes after the rooms were darkened. Others tucked it into their underwear. Women wore bulky bloomers in Duncan's day, much roomier underwear than the garments worn today. They made it easy to hide things—and easy to pull them out at just the right moment.

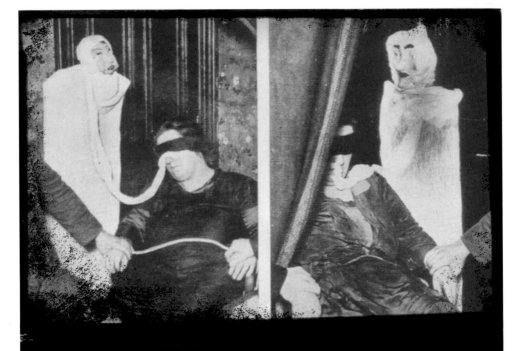

These photos revealed Helen Duncan as a fraud. In a darkened room, these handmade "ghosts" deceived many who wanted to believe they were hearing from a loved one. Harvey Metcalfe took these photos in 1928 at a séance held at Duncan's house.

When Duncan claimed to produce a filmy substance at séance after séance, Harry Price, director of Britain's National Laboratory of Psychical Research, took notice and challenged her to prove the stuff scientifically. Price, once an avid student of magic, had become an expert at debunking false spiritualists, including the fraudulent "spirit" photographer William Hope in 1922. With the cooperation of the University of London, Price established the National Laboratory of Psychical Research to continue his investigative work.

Duncan agreed to Price's tests in October 1931. She allowed medical personnel to conduct a thorough body search prior to each controlled séance. She also agreed to wear special fraud-proof clothing. Price suspected she swallowed the ectoplasmic material and later threw it up in the darkness of the room. When he asked her to let them take an X-ray, Duncan refused and ran from the test location in a panic.

In 1939 Price got his confirmation when a lengthy piece of her "ectoplasm" was confiscated for analysis at one of her last séances. Duncan's ectoplasm consisted of several yards of cheesecloth stained with blood.

Duncan was declared a fraud and convicted under the United Kingdom's Witchcraft Act, in effect since 1735. She served nine months in prison.

JOE NICKELL, MODERN-DAY SKEPTIC

For forty years, Joe Nickell searched for explanations to prove that people's ghostly claims are really their misunderstanding of natural phenomenon. He's written about his investigations in dozens of books and in the magazine *Skeptical Inquirer.*

He didn't start out being skeptical. He grew up an ordinary kid in West Liberty, Kentucky, curious about the natural world and all things supernatural. "I dreamed of being a magician. I dreamed of being an investigator. I dreamed of being a lot of things," he explains. "And eventually, I became most of them." As a former magician with a PhD in literary investigation and folklore—and as an expert in proving historical documents are real—Nickell is used to things both fictional and factual. And ghosts, according to Nickell, just don't add up.

"Much of what so-called ghost hunters are detecting is themselves," he says. "If they go through a haunted house and stir up dust, they shouldn't be surprised if they get a lot of orbs in their photographs." According to Nickell, all photographic orbs are dust particles out of focus. He believes other bits of evidence can be explained just as easily. He's especially suspicious of mediums for one reason: the messages they share are too ordinary.

"If they've [spirits] crossed to the other side," Nickell asks, "why don't they have anything meaningful to say? And if they do, for heaven's sake, why don't they speak up?"

Most of the time, Nickell finds a natural explanation for weird events. "I'm not saying there's a fifty-fifty chance there's a ghost in that haunted house," he says. "I think the chances are closer to 99.9 percent there isn't. But let's go look. We might learn something interesting."

CHAPTER FIVE

PARANORMAL EXPERIENCES

W hile working on this book, I've conducted research with an open but skeptical mind. Most of what I've discovered has been interesting but not very convincing. For example, cold spots inside a bedroom turned out to be drafts of air coming from the frosty skylight just outside the bedroom door. Creaking floors were evidence of old, weathered houses, not hauntings. Debunking the so-called proof of ghosts was relatively easy, in most cases.

But every now and then, I found a story so gripping I couldn't sweep it away like an old cobweb. I wondered, *Is it possible a part of us does survive after the body dies? And can that energy reach out to loved ones who are still living?* Some of the experiences in this chapter made me think that maybe, just maybe, the answer is yes.

You'll have to decide whether you agree with me. You can do your own research and use critical thinking to make up your mind.

POINT-AND-SHOOT GHOST MYSTERY

Author Vivian Vande Velde does not believe in ghosts. She writes about them, but she says they live only in her vivid imagination. She does have a ghostly mystery to solve, though. In a photo she took, who or what is that figure behind her friend?

On March 6, 2005, Vande Velde and her friend were at a literature festival in Missouri. Using an ordinary point-and-shoot digital camera, Vande Velde took two back-to-back pictures of Angie sitting in a folding chair. No one was standing behind her when the flash went off either time. Three days passed before Vande Velde uploaded her photos to her computer. When she did, she was puzzled. Angie was smiling, all alone, in the first shot. In the second, taken only seconds later, a translucent boy is standing behind her.

Was it a boy's reflection captured on the glass behind Angie? No, Vande Velde remembers, because there was no reflective surface behind her friend. Did the boy photobomb (run in, pose in the background, and then run out) Vande Velde's picture? Again, she says no. No one was anywhere near where Angie was sitting.

Could the image of the boy be a ghostly apparition? Vande Velde doubts it. "People have been dying for centuries. If they all became ghosts, they would outnumber living people, and we'd all have paranormal experiences."

On the other hand, Vande Velde admits, it's not impossible. "I don't know everything, and just because I can't imagine it, doesn't mean it isn't so. It's interesting to speculate about ghosts, about someone's spirit continuing after death."

It'll take a lot more than one mysterious photo to convince Vande Velde that ghosts exist.

Take a close look at the boy in the picture on the right. What do you think—is he a ghost, or did something else happen?

Bumps in the Night

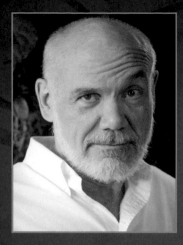

A common sign that a spirit is sharing a home is sounds: soft singing from the attic, footsteps on the stairs, knocks and wraps that cannot be explained. Author Bruce Coville is famous for his spine-chilling fiction, but his real-life story offers a perfect example of ghosts that go bump in the night. He wanted to share this story with you in this book.

I was, for many years, a gravedigger, but I never had a sense of being in the presence of a spirit while I worked in the cemetery. Nor did I ever see the ghost that everyone claimed haunted the theater where I sometimes performed. Only once have I had the sense of a spirit's presence. My wife and I were living in what had been a farmhand's house in a rural area of southern New York State.

On the first floor of the house were a kitchen, a living room, and a small room. Upstairs were two rooms: our bedroom and a workroom. That was it—a very limited space.

Late one night, the phone rang and terrible news arrived. A friend had died unexpectedly. She had been a funny, vibrant, intensely alive person—so her death was not only sad but shocking.

I turned to tell my wife. As I did, we both heard, clearly and distinctly, footsteps crossing the floor in the room above our heads. We were alone in an isolated house out in the country. Eyes wide, we looked at each other and had the same thought: Our friend had come to bid us farewell.

I went upstairs to check, but no one and nothing was there—no possible source for those very clear footsteps.

No possible source except a visiting spirit.

AN ODD-FELLOW HANGING

Do ghosts wander the halls of the Odd Fellows Home in Liberty, Missouri? According to its new owners—who have turned it into the Belvoir Winery—the answer is yes.

Not everyone meets the ghosts. Some people just tour the vineyards. Others pose for wedding photographs in front of the buildings of vivid red bricks. But the estate was not always so romantic.

The Independent Order of Odd Fellows, a service group committed to caring for the poor, bought the place in 1890. At the time, it was a three-year-old luxury hotel. The Odd Fellows converted it to a home for orphaned children and elderly people. The able-bodied residents worked on the farm to earn their keep. Whenever a resident passed away, the Odd Fellows buried him or her in the adjacent private cemetery.

Mischievous spirits allegedly haunt the Belvoir Winery, once known as the Odd Fellows Home, in Liberty, Missouri.

Eventually the Odd Fellows home was closed. In the late 1990s, Dr. John L. Bean and his wife planted a vineyard and built the Belvoir Winery on the site. Almost immediately, employees experienced things no one could explain.

Chris Choice, a physical education teacher in the area, works part-time at the winery, primarily helping with renovations. When his son Connor needed a summer job, Choice got him to pitch in.

According to Choice, the main winery building was once the Odd Fellows orphanage. One day, Connor was working alone at 8:00 a.m., cleaning the front staircase windows. When Connor got to the second-floor landing—a space roughly 8 by 15 feet (2 by 5 m)—he ran out of paper towels. He set his bottle of cleaning fluid on the stairs and walked to the storage area to get more towels. When he returned, the bottle had vanished. Puzzled, he turned to go back downstairs for a new bottle. Then he saw it.

The cleaning fluid bottle was hanging from the chandelier in the middle of the main entrance. It was 9 feet (3 m) off the floor.

Connor thought it was a practical joke. He called out to whoever was messing around.

When his dad arrived forty-five minutes later, Connor was waiting outside the building. He told his father what had happened. They went inside, and Choice saw the bottle with his own eyes. "The hair on the back of my neck was sticking straight up the whole time we were in the building," Choice says.

Connor asked his father to admit he'd sneaked in to pull this prank. But Choice was adamant. "I hadn't even left home when it happened," he explains. When two other workers arrived at 11:00 a.m., Connor quizzed them too. But like Choice, they had been nowhere near the winery. It took a tall ladder to retrieve the bottle.

"Connor finished the summer working at the estate," Choice says. "But he would never work alone in that building again." The mystery was never solved. Ghostly mischief seemed to be the only possible explanation.

WHY ARE YOU CRYING?

Teacher and librarian Kyra Richardson will never forget something that happened when her son, Nakoa, was just an infant. "I was in the attic of our 1910 home, the same house my husband grew up in," Kyra recalls. Her husband was away, and she'd put baby Nakoa to bed moments earlier.

"Nakoa was about a year old and in his crib on the first floor," she says. "He was crying, but I had already fed him and changed his diaper; I had rocked him and put him down. I was trying to let him learn to soothe himself to sleep." So, she turned on the baby monitor in his room, closed the door, and listened to his soft cries from her monitor in the attic.

"Suddenly, over the baby monitor, I heard a child's voice say, 'Why are you crying?' And Nakoa immediately stopped."

"I knew nobody else could be in the house. The doors were locked, and the old house was creaky. If anyone had come in, I would have heard it. I was totally freaked out."

Her heart pounding, Richardson rushed downstairs and opened the door, not knowing what she'd find. There was Nakoa, wide-awake, completely calm, and alone.

"My husband had told me about his own encounters in the house," Richardson says. "But I never believed him until that day."

Life went on. The Richardson family outgrew the haunted house, but Richardson never forgot the voice that defied earthly explanation.

VOICES IN THE DARK

Field research is an important part of writing a nonfiction book, especially one about ghosts. So I traveled to five states to explore haunted places. Most were fun to visit but offered very little paranormal activity. However, a few yielded evidence I cannot debunk or explain, including the William Heath Davis House in San Diego, California.

San Diego paranormal investigators Colleen Rose and Maritza Scandunas met me and my team—photographer Roxyanne Young and her fifteen-year-old daughter, Danielle—at 9:30 p.m. for an evening of professional ghost hunting. Except for the light from miniature flashlights Rose and Scandunas held, every inch of the old house was dark. Wooden floorboards creaked and moaned under the weight of our footsteps. Every room was filled with musty-smelling antique furniture and keepsakes, including the living room, where our investigation began.

Because most of the thirty ghosts allegedly haunting the house were male and because Danielle was not part of the professional team, Rose asked if she wanted to use the dowsing rods to ask a few yes-or-no questions. If the hovering bars crossed, she explained, the spirits would be answering yes. If they did not cross, the answer would be no.

"Kelly, what question would you like to ask?" Rose asked me.

"Ask them if it's a good idea for me to write a ghost book for kids," I replied.

Danielle softly asked my question, and slowly, the two bars crossed. "Whoa!" she whispered.

"Now ask them to uncross the bars," Rose said, "so we can ask more questions." Danielle did, and almost immediately, the bars uncrossed. Rose asked if we were talking to the doctor, and the bars were still. She asked Danielle to ask who we were talking with, hoping the ghost's answer might register on the digital recorder. Danielle did. The bars did not waver.

Scandunas rewound her digital recorder to where the dowsing-rod session had begun. With a click in the dark, she played it back. We heard the sound track of the moments we had just experienced, including Danielle's last question. We hadn't heard anything else at the time, so I expected silence. I was stunned to hear a male voice whisper, "Stephen."

Rose and Scandunas laughed because they recognized Stephen, the ghost of a Civil War soldier they'd encountered at the house on previous ghost hunts. "No wonder," they said. "Stephen can never resist a pretty girl's question."

Next, we climbed the stairs and moved to a bedroom on the second level. "It's

Danielle Ohumukini *(center)* and the San Diego Ghost Hunters reach out to spirits believed to haunt the William Davis House.

George's room," Scandunas explained. He was a precise, old businessman who'd died of natural causes in the house in the 1940s.

An hour passed. The ghost hunters used their Ovilus, a kind of "word box." In theory, the entities can use their electrical energy to prompt a word to be emitted from a tiny speaker. Many words flowed out of the box, but most were garbled. Then three words came out: "Whaley," "Jim," and "hanged."

The hair on my arms stood up. Was it just a coincidence that I had visited San Diego's haunted Whaley House the day before? Legend had it that Yankee Jim had been hanged from a tree where the Whaley House now stood. How would *these* spirits know where I'd been yesterday?

Then the box went quiet. Scandunas explained we were about to leave the bedroom to move down to the kitchen. She asked, "George, is there anything you need?" When she immediately played back her digital recorder, I clearly heard her voice ask the question. A male voice responded, "Send them home, yes?" According to Scandunas, George had grown tired of a room full of strangers. So we said good-bye and went to the kitchen.

Rose and Scandunas opened a zippered bag in the first-floor kitchen and revealed a small collection of toys. They scattered miniature cars, stuffed animals, and picture books across the kitchen as we settled on the cold wooden floor. Rose explained that the house's ghost children loved to play in the kitchen.

Almost nothing happened for the next hour as we tried to reach out to the kids. Then Rose asked Danielle to read the animal picture book aloud. When Danielle finished, Rose asked any ghosts present, "Did you see all the colorful pictures?" When she played back her recorder, a child's voice exclaimed, "I seen 'em!" We were delighted.

Before I left, I wrote down the make and the model of their digital recorders and asked if they could send me the voice files. I bought the same recorder and later shared the sound files with an audio expert at my local television station. He confessed he did not believe in ghosts, but he said he knew of no way to fake voices on a digital recorder. He said any attempt to layer sounds would simply erase the first, leaving only the second recording.

Did three different ghosts respond to our questions at the William Heath Davis House? Or did sound waves from nearby radio or television transmissions show up on the digital recorders at just the right moments, accidentally conveying just the right messages? It's hard to say. But, I confess, I was astonished.

If ghosts are real, if they truly linger in old, haunted houses, this might be the way they entertain themselves, by playing with would-be ghost hunters. Nothing would surprise me now.

CONCLUSION

I have to admit, before I wrote this book, I was a little bit scared of ghosts. I'd heard stories of evil energy and angry spirits. I'd seen movies and read books about mean ghosts that did harmful things to people. The thought of delving into information about these entities made me uneasy. I definitely didn't want to make one angry with me. But after four years of research, my focus has shifted.

The author at Yankee Jim's grave site by the Whaley House in San Diego, California

Overall, I'm still a skeptic—mainly because I didn't find any hard proof of their existence. I did hear mysterious voices on digital recorders that seemed to be talking to me. But not one ghost tried to push me down a flight of stairs. Not one threatened to possess or terrify me. I saw no evidence that any spirit being meant any harm to any person. I didn't see any apparitions or smell my mom's gingerbread again.

That doesn't mean others haven't had those kinds of experiences. I think some witnesses are credible. My opinion, based on my research, is that there is a good chance ghosts are real—but if they are, they don't seem to be dangerous. When I actually stepped into those so-called haunted places, fear never crossed my mind—amazement often did.

Being cautious is never a bad thing. It's an instinct designed to protect us from danger. By all means, be careful in any adventures you decide to undertake. But be open to possibilities and wonder. For me, wonder usually wins out in the end. I'll remain skeptical—but I won't stop searching for answers to things I don't understand.

Happy hauntings, whatever you decide.

HOW PEOPLE FAKE GHOST PHOTOS

Some ghost photographs may be authentic evidence of the afterlife. But most are not. Some are photographs of natural things misunderstood, like fog or flying insects. Some are deliberately faked by photographers trying to deceive unsuspecting viewers. Professional photographer Roxyanne Young, who documented several of my ghost-hunting field trips, also prepared these instructions to help you understand how dishonest people try to fool you. If you know how photos are faked, you'll be able to tell when some of them might be real.

#1: A GHOST IN THE GROUP

Equipment:

1. a DSLR camera

2. friend dressed in old-fashioned clothes

3. friends dressed in modern clothes

4. tripod

Using a tripod to hold the camera steady, point it at a group of friends.
NOTE: A flash is not used on this shot.

1. The DSLR mode is set to "M" for manual.

2. The shutter speed is set to five seconds.

3. The ISO and f-stop are adjusted so the exposure will be correct. These will depend on the setting and the amount of ambient light in the room.

4. The photographer clicks the shutter release button and has the "ghost model" walk quickly into the frame near the group of people, stop and stare into the lens for a count of three, and then walk back out of the frame quickly.

The trick is to make sure no one in the group moves for the whole five seconds. If they move, they'll be blurry and the photo will look faked. The "ghost" has to walk in and out QUICKLY. In quick; stop; stare and count 1, 2, 3 and out FAST.

What you get looks something like the image on the next page.

What looks like a ghost may be just a clever camera trick.

#2: SPIRIT ORBS

Equipment:

1. a camera with a flash
2. a spray bottle filled with water
3. 2 to 3 tablespoons (30 to 44 milliliters) of dish soap

One of the classic "ghost" images involves little balls of light that some believe is a form of spirit energy. To fake these, a person puts 2 or 3 tablespoons of dish soap into a spray bottle filled with water. It is NOT shaken, because the photographer doesn't want bubbles. They are aiming for a soapy coating on the water droplets.

The camera is set up with the flash ON. This works best at night with a dark background. Someone spritzes some soapy water into the air, and the photographer clicks the shutter release on the camera. The flash will capture water droplets in the air, and the soapy coating on the droplets will look like glowing orbs. Sometimes, a face is reflected in an orb, making the photo even more "ghostly."

SOURCE NOTES

7   Lee Spiegel, "Spooky Number of Americans Believe in Ghosts," *Huffington Post,* February 2, 2013, http://www.huffingtonpost.com/2013/02/02/real-ghosts-americans-poll_n_2049485.html.

8   "Medium—Allison DuBois Interview, Part 1," YouTube video, 2:09, posted by "3NG7AND", March 18, 2007, http://www.youtube.com/watch?v=5okOKdNqxw4&list=PLFB535575C2AEFF5.

9–10 Mark Hunnemann, *Seeing Ghosts through God's Eyes* (Lake Placid, NY: Aviva, 2010), Kindle edition.

11 Danielle Ohumukini, interview with the author, September 22, 2013.

11 Brian Dunning, "Orbs: The Ghosts in the Camera," *Skeptoids.com,* February 24, 2007, http://skeptoid.com/episodes/4029.

12 Michael Walsh, "Louisiana Reporter Purportedly Captures Footage of Ghost…," *New York Daily News*, December 13, 2012, http://www.nydailynews.com/news/national/reporter-films-ghost-la-plantation-article-1.1219737.

13 Dave Juliano, "What Is a Residual Haunting?," *The Shadow Lands,* 2012, accessed January 22, 2014, http://theshadowlands.net/ghost/residual.htm.

14 Kelly Milner Halls, "A Dog? A Cat? That's a Ghost, Buster!," *Chicago Tribune,* October 20, 1998, D8, http://articles.chicagotribune.com/1998-10-20/features/9810200057_1_cat-real-life-ghostbuster-animals.

14 Katherine Faulkner, "Ghost of the Dambusters Dog: Picture Shows Long-Dead Labrador at Memorial to WWII Heroes," *Daily Mail* (UK), November 2, 2011, http://www.dailymail.co.uk/news/article-2056353/Dambusters-dog-ghost-Picture-shows-long-dead-labrador-WWII-memorial.html.

14 Ibid.

15 Jamie Jackson, "Pennies from Heaven," *Gettysburg Ghosts,* January 22, 2013, http://gburgghosts.blogspot.com/2013/01/pennies-from-heaven.html.

19 Lisa Yee, original essay, October 5, 2013.

21 Chris Gray Faust, "Welcome to Hotel Paranormal," *USA Today,* January 24, 2013, accessed January 22, 2014, http://www.usatoday.com/story/travel/hotels/2013/01/24/stanley-hotel-stephen-king-the-shining-estes-park-colorado/1861153.

21 Doug Clark, "Davenport Ghost Has Roots in Fact," *Spokesman-Review,* August 18, 2005, http://www.spokesman.com/stories/2005/aug/18/davenport-ghost-has-roots-in-fact.

22 Ibid.

22 Phil Keller, "Gettysburg, PA," *The Shadowlands*, n.d., accessed April 15, 2014, http://theshadowlands.net/famous/gettysburg.htm.

23 "Revisiting the Haunted History of Gettysburg," *Economist/Intelligent Life,* October 17, 2008, accessed January 22, 2014, http://moreintelligentlife.com/story/american-ghosts.

24 "The Alamo," *Weird U.S.,* n.d., accessed April 15, 2014, http://www.weirdus.com/states/texas/ghosts/alamo/index.php.

24 "Bachelors Grove Cemetery—Illinois (Travel Channel)." YouTube video, 4:52, posted by "AfterDeathParanormal," January 19, 2011, http://www.youtube.com/watch?feature=player_embedded&v=fto8QGqJraI#t=80.

24–25 Jason Sullivan, e-mail interview with the author, September 29, 2013.

25 Jonathan Turley, "Giles Corey: An Iron Man Who Was a Victim of the Salem Witch Hysteria," *Jonathan Turley Blog,* October 1, 2010, 2014, http://jonathanturley.org/2010/10/30/giles-corey-an-iron-man-who-was-a-victim-of-the-salem-witch-hysteria.

26 Joann Hoxha, interview with the author, January 22, 2014, and blog, http://halloweenezine.wordpress.com/tag/ghost-hunters.

27 Rachel S. Johnstone, *Inmates of the Idaho State Penitentiary: 1864 to 1947* (Boise: Idaho Historical Society, 2008), 12, accessed January 22, 2014, http://history.idaho.gov/sites/default/files/uploads/inmates_1864-1947.pdf.

34 Shane McCorristine, "The Case of Nickoli and Spectral Illusion Theory," *WellcomeHistory.com,* July 22, 2010, http://wellcomehistory.wordpress.com/2010/07/22/the-case-of-nicolai-and-spectral-illusions-theory.

39 Alane Ferguson, interview with the author, June 19, 2013.

40 Daniel Bubbeo, "'Long Island Medium' Theresa Caputo Returns with new Season and Book, 'There's More to Life Than This,'" *Newsday,* September 25, 2013, http://www.newsday.com/entertainment/tv/reality-tv/long-island-medium-theresa-caputo-returns-with-new-season-and-book-there-s-more-to-life-than-this-1.6137483.

40 "The Sixth Sense: The Performers." YouTube video, 2:35, posted by "ABC News," October 26, 2012, https://www.youtube.com/watch?v=YnJ4wT2mKJ4.

40 Theresa Caputo, "Theresa Caputo Live Show," INB Performing Arts Center, Spokane, WA, June 14, 2013.

42 Karen Abbott, "The Fox Sisters and the Rap on Spiritualism," *Smithsonian Magazine,* October 30, 2012, http://www.smithsonianmag.com/history/the-fox-sisters-and-the-rap-on-spiritualism-99663697/?no-ist.

45 Harry Houdini, *A Magician among the Spirits* (New York: Arno Press, 1972), 5. First published 1924 by Harper & Brothers.

45 Ryan Munshower and Angelica W. Capone, "Channeling Houdini in Scranton," *Pennsylvania for the Book,* spring 2011, accessed April 15, 2014, http://pabook.libraries.psu.edu/palitmap/Houdini.html.

45 Daniel Kraker, "Houdini Relative Unlocks Some Family Secrets," *NPR,* October 31, 2011, http://www.npr.org/2011/10/31/141366283/houdini-relative-unlocks-some-family-secrets.

47 Burkhard Bilger, "Waiting for Ghosts," *New Yorker,* December 23, 2012, http://www.newyorker.com/archive/2002/12/23/021223fa_fact_bilger.

50 Vivian Van Velde, interview with the author, June 13, 2013.

51 Bruce Coville, original essay, September 23, 2013.

53 Chris Choice, interview with the author, January 14, 2014.

53 Kyra Richardson, interview with the author, February 14, 2014.

54-56 Ohumukini, interview with the author.

GLOSSARY

apparition: a ghost that appears as a see-through human form

charlatan: a false expert; one who claims knowledge or gifts he or she does not have

devastate: greatly upset

devout: very religious or devoted to something

disembodied: freed from the physical body

dowsing rods: (also known as divining rods) two narrow poles used to detect sources of water

DSLR: digital single-lens reflex, a type of camera

electronic voice phenomena (EVP): sounds resembling speech that are found on tape recorders and other electronic devices, often thought to be the voices of spirits

entities: beings

escape artist: an entertainer who frees himself from chains, boxes, or other "impossible" restraints

exorcise: to free a person or place from evil

falsified: to make something fake; to con people into believing something that isn't true

fanatical: having excessive excitement or interest in a person or subject

gallows: a frame for hanging criminals

hereafter: after death

hoax: a purposeful deception

imperial: of empire or emperor; supremely powerful

infrared: a portion of light spectrum invisible to the naked eye

magnate: a wealthy and powerful businessperson

medium: a person who claims to communicate with the dead

mortuary: a place where dead bodies are prepared for burial

paranormal: impossible to explain scientifically; beyond normal

penitentiary: a prison

profiler: someone who studies people's behavior, usually with the aim of unmasking criminals or frauds

reenactors: people who dress in historic-styled clothing to act out historic events

residual: left over or left behind

scholar: a person who has done advanced study in a certain field

séance: a gathering of people to talk to the dead

spiritualist: a person who believes the dead communicate with the living

translucent: transparent enough to let through some light

tripod: a three-legged stand for cameras or telescopes

vague: unclear

SELECTED BIBLIOGRAPHY

Caputo, Theresa. *There's More to Life Than This: Healing Messages, Remarkable Stories, and Insight about the Other Side from the Long Island Medium*. New York: Astria, 2013.

Danmar, William. *Ghostology: Products of Nature; the Naturalistic Philosophy of the Ghosts*. New York: Danmar, 1924.

DuBois, Allison. *We Are Their Heaven: Why the Dead Never Leave Us*. New York: Simon & Schuster, 2006.

Hill, Kathy Deinhardt. *Hanged: A History of Idaho's Executions*. McCall, ID: Bob Mallard, 2010.

Nickell, Joe. *The Science of Ghosts: Searching for Spirits of the Dead*. Amherst, NY: Prometheus, 2012.

Roach, Mary. *Spook*. New York: W. W. Norton & Co., 2005.

Weisberg, Barbara. *Talking to the Dead: Kate and Maggie Fox and the Rise of Spiritualism*. San Francisco: HarperSanFrancisco, 2004.

FURTHER READING

BOOKS

Ballard, Robert, and Rick Archbold. *Ghost Liners: Exploring the World's Greatest Lost Ships.* New York: Little, Brown, 1998.

Bingham, Jane. *Ghosts and Haunted Houses.* London: Raintree, 2013.

Bridges, Shirin Yim. *Horrible Hauntings: An Augmented Reality Collection of Ghosts and Ghouls.* Foster City, CA: Goosebottom Books, 2012.

Gee, Joshua. *Encyclopedia Horrifica.* New York: Scholastic, 2007.

Hawes, Jason, and Grant Wilson. *Ghost Hunt: Chilling Tales of the Unknown.* New York: Little, Brown, 2010.

———. *Ghost Hunt 2: More Chilling Tales of the Unknown.* New York: Little, Brown, 2011.

WEBSITES

Ghost Doctors Ghost Tours of NYC
http://ghostdoctors.com

Ghost Hunters of Texas
http://ghosthuntersoftexas.com

Ohio Ghost Hunters: EVP Investigations
http://www.evpinvestigations.com

Rocky Mountain Paranormal Research Society
http://www.rockymountainparanormal.com

San Diego Ghost Hunters
http://www.sandiegoghosthunters.com

TAPS
http://www.the-atlantic-paranormal-society.com

PLACES TO VISIT

HAUNTED HOUSES

Brumder Mansion :: Milwaukee, WI
http://milwaukeebedbreakfast.com

Franklin Castle :: Cleveland, OH
http://www.deadohio.com/franklincastle.htm

Wayne Gordan House :: Savannah, GA
http://www.juliettegordonlowbirthplace.org
/site-history/the-wayne-gordon-house

Whaley House :: San Diego, CA
http://whaleyhouse.org

HAUNTED HOTELS

Davenport Hotel :: Spokane, WA
http://www.davenporthotelcollection.com

Hotel del Coronado :: Coronado, CA
http://www.hoteldel.com

Menger Hotel :: San Antonio, TX
http://www.mengerhotel.com

Spalding Inn :: Whitefield, NH
http://www.thespaldinginn.com

HAUNTED HISTORIC BATTLE AREAS

The Alamo :: San Antonio, TX
http://thealamo.org

Colonial National Historic Park/
Yorktown Battlefield :: Yorktown, VA
http://www.nps.gov.yonb/index.htm

Gettysburg National Military Park ::
Gettysburg, PA
http://www.nps.gov/gett/index.htm

Little Bighorn Battlefield National Monument
:: Crow Agency, MT
http://www.nps.gov/libi/historyculture
/index.htm

Pearl Harbor :: Honolulu, HI
http://www.pearlharboroahu.com

HAUNTED CEMETERIES

Boothill Graveyard :: Tombstone, AZ
http://www.boothillgraves.com

El Campo Santo Cemetery :: San Diego, CA
http://gothere.com/sandiego/Ghosts/El_
Campo_Santo/default.htm

Howard Street Cemetery :: Salem, MA
http://www.graveaddiction.com
/howardst.html

St. Louis Cemetery 1 :: New Orleans, LA
http://www.saveourcemeteries.org
/st-louis-cemetery-no-1

HAUNTED PRISONS

Alcatraz Island :: San Francisco, CA
http://www.nps.gov/alca/index.htm

Burlington County Prison Museum :: Mount
Holly, NJ
http://www.prisonmuseum.net

Eastern State Penitentiary :: Philadelphia, PA
http://www.easternstate.org

Moundsfield West Virginia Penitentiary ::
Moundsfield, WV
http://www.wvpentours.com

HAUNTED SHIPS

Delta King :: Old Sacramento, CA
http://deltaking.com

Queen Mary :: Long Beach, CA
http://www.queenmary.com/attractions
-events/haunted-encounters.php

Star of India :: San Diego, CA
http://www.sdmaritime.org

USS Hornet :: Alameda, CA
http://www.uss-hornet.org

USS North Carolina :: Wilmington, NC
http://www.battleshipnc.com

INDEX

PHOTO ACKNOWLEDGMENTS

The images in this book are used with the permission of: © iStockphoto.com/Ivan Bliznetsov, p. 1; © iStockphoto.com/gschroer, pp. 1, 2–6, 16–17, 32, 33, 41, 48–49, 57 (background); © Diane Diederich/E+/Getty Images, p. 4; © iStockphoto.com/DavidMSchrader, pp. 4, 6, 16, 32, 48 (black frame); © iStockphoto.com/grapix, p. 6; © iStockphoto.com/upheaval, pp. 8–15, 18–31, 34–40, 42–47, 50–56, 58–64 (sketchy border); © iStockphoto.com/aldra, pp. 8, 14, 19, 36, 37, 39, 51 (green background); © iStockphoto.com/Gordan1, pp. 8–13, 15, 18, 20–31, 34–35, 38–40, 42–47, 50–56, 58–64 (grunge frame); Library of Congress HABS NJ,3-MOUHO,8—3, p. 9; © iStockphoto.com/cla78, pp. 9, 10, 18, 21, 29, 30, 35, 38, 46, 50, 52 (black and white frames); Photo by Roxyanne Young, pp. 10, 37, 55, 57, 59; © Lisa B. Davis, p. 12; © Daily Mail/Rex/Alamy, p. 14; © iStockphoto.com /catscandotcom, p. 16; Earl S. Cryer/ZUMAPRESS.COM/Newscom, p. 18; Courtesy of Lisa Yee, p. 19; © Nomadic Lass/flickr.com, p. 20; © David Fulmer/flickr.com, p. 21; Library of Congress LC-B811-234, p. 23; © Antonio Bovino/flickr.com, p. 25; © Boston Globe via Getty Images, p. 26; Photographs in the Carol M. Highsmith Archive/Library of Congress/LC-DIG-highsm-8110, p. 28; National Archives 5900075, p. 29; © Anthony Dunn/Alamy, p. 30; © iStockphoto.com/inhauscreative, p. 32; © Syfy/NBCU Photo Bank/Getty Images, p. 35; © Greg Wahl-Stephens/AP/CORBIS, p. 38; Missouri History Museum, St. Louis, photo by Thomas M. Easterly n17196, p. 42; From the Lincoln Financial Foundation Collection, courtesy of the Indiana State Museum and Historic Sites, p. 43; Library of Congress LC-USZ62-99116, p. 44; Wikimedia Commons, p. 46; © iStockphoto.com/gmnicholas, p. 48; © Vivian Vande Velde, p. 50; © Sonya Sones, p. 51; © Kelly Milner Halls, p. 52.

Front Cover: © Estelle Lagarde/Millennium Images, UK.
Back Cover: © Giorgio Fochesato/Vetta/Getty Images; Jacket flaps: The George F. Landegger Collection of Alabama Photographs in Carol M. Highsmith›s America, Library of Congress LC-DIG-highsm-06441.

Tualatin Public Library
18878 SW Martinazzi Avenue
Tualatin, OR 97062-7092
Member of Washington County Cooperative Library Services